HANDBOOK

Horses & Ponies

Written by

Camille de le Bedoyere

First published in 2009 by Miles Kelly Publishing Ltd
Harding's Barn, Bardfield End Green, Thaxted, Essex, CM6 3PX, UK

This edition printed in 2013

2 4 6 8 10 9 7 5 3 1

Publishing Director Belinda Gallagher
Creative Director Jo Brewer
Assistant Editor Carly Blake
Cover Designer Jo Cowan
Designer Joe Jones
Image Manager Lorraine King
Production Manager Elizabeth Collins
Reprographics Stephan Davis, Thom Allaway
Archive Manager Jennifer Hunt

ISBN 978-1-78209-165-3

Printed in China

British Library Cataloguing-in-Publication Data
A catalogue record for this book is available from the British Library

Made with paper from a sustainable forest

www.mileskelly.net
info@mileskelly.net

www.factsforprojects.com

CONTENTS

INTRODUCTION

Horses and ponies are fascinating animals. They can be graceful, gentle and tame, yet incredibly strong and full of energy. Learning about these wonderful animals can be the beginning of a journey that grows into a lifetime of discovery.

Family matters

Horses and ponies belong to a group of animals called equids, which also includes zebras and donkeys. Members of this group have a single toe on each foot called a hoof. Equids are intelligent animals that like to live in groups called herds.

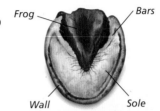

Frog
Bars
Wall
Sole

◄ Hooves are made from keratin – the same material found in your fingernails. When horseshoes are fitted, they are nailed to the wall of the hoof.

Donkey

Horses

Zebras

What is a breed?

Types of horse or pony that share similar characteristics such as size and strength are called a 'breed'. Arab, Shire and Shetland are all examples of breeds. Horses are also divided into three groups – hotbloods, warmbloods and coldbloods.

Shetland

TYPES OF HORSE

Hotbloods

These are the fastest runners and are often used for racing. They are high-spirited and can be difficult to handle.

Arab

Warmbloods

Warmblooded horses were bred by crossing hotbloods with the large, heavy coldbloods of northern Europe. They are good runners, but are sturdier and calmer than hotbloods.

Camargues

Coldbloods

These calm, gentle horses are large and strong. They were used for pulling heavy loads and farm work. Coldbloods are also known as heavy horses or draught horses.

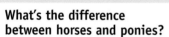

Shires

What's the difference between horses and ponies?

The main difference is that ponies are usually smaller than horses. They also have shorter legs and may have long, feathery fur around their hooves. Their tails and manes are often thicker than horses. Many types of pony are known for their calm, patient natures. Falabellas are the smallest breed of pony standing around just 32 inches tall.

Arabian horse

Falabella pony

ANATOMY

The parts of a horse's or pony's body that you can see have been given names, called 'points'. Some are similar to those we use to name our own body parts, but some of them are quite different. The points are useful when talking about the appearance of horses and ponies, how to look after them and how to ride, so it is useful to learn the points and where they are.

POINTS OF A HORSE

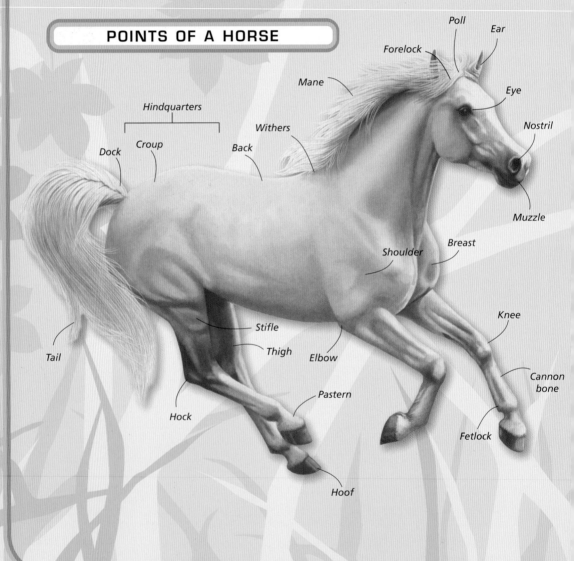

Poll

Ear

Forelock

Eye

Mane

Nostril

Hindquarters

Withers

Muzzle

Dock

Croup

Back

Breast

Shoulder

Knee

Stifle

Cannon bone

Tail

Thigh

Elbow

Pastern

Hock

Fetlock

Hoof

Shape and build

The shape and build of horses' and ponies' bodies is called their conformation. This includes the size of their bones and muscles. Conformation varies depending on the breed and different conformations are good for different skills. Some horses and ponies are more suited to fast running or showjumping than others. A good conformation includes a neck that is about one-third of the animal's total length, a small head and large, clear eyes.

Up to 6 months   *5 years old*

15 years old   *25 years old*

Teeth

As horses and ponies get older their teeth wear down and become more triangular in shape. Experts can guess a horse's or pony's age by looking at the length and shape of its teeth. The teeth at the front, called incisors, are used for cutting and slicing grass.

Measuring height

The height of a horse or pony is measured from the ground to the base of its neck, called its withers.

When people first began measuring the heights of horses and ponies they used their hands as units of measurement. A 'hand' – the width of an average man's hand – is four inches, or 10 centimetres. If the animal measures more than an exact number of hands, the extra measurement is given in inches after a decimal point. A height of 12 hands and one inch is written as 12.1 hh (hands high).

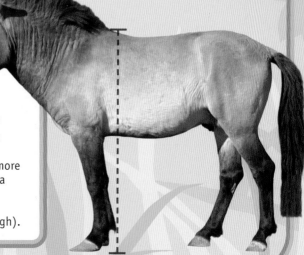

COLOURS AND MARKINGS

Horses and ponies are often described by the colour of their coat and the markings on their body. This can be used to identify them. Horses' and ponies' coats come in a wide range of colours and patterns, but few are described as white, instead they are called grey.

Black Pure black colouring is rare as most black types have some brown or white hairs. Friesian horses are pure black.

Black

Chestnut Fur is reddish-brown all over and points (mane, tail, ears and lower legs) are a similar colour, without any black.

Chestnut

Brown

Brown Coat is dark brown all over, including points.

Grey

Grey Horses and ponies that have lots of white in their coats are described as grey. They appear slightly grey because their dark skin shows through.

Palomino Fur is golden all over, and the tail and mane should be white or flaxen (pale yellow). They have white socks and may have small white markings on their faces.

Palomino

Roan Strawberry roans have chestnut fur with white hair growing through, giving them a pink tinge. Blue roans have black fur with white hairs, giving a slightly blue appearance.

Strawberry roan

Bay

Dun

Dun The body is pale golden and the mane and tail are black. Duns also have eel stripes along their backs (see page 9).

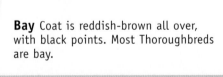

Bay Coat is reddish-brown all over, with black points. Most Thoroughbreds are bay.

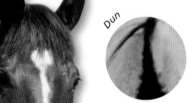

Part-coloureds These horses and ponies have large patches of fur of different colours. Animals with black and white patches are called Piebald. Those that have brown and white patches are called Skewbald. Spotted horses and ponies have dabs of light fur on a dark coat or dark dabs on a pale coat. The Appaloosa is an American breed of horse that is famous for its variety of spotted coat patterns.

Spotted

Piebald

Skewbald

Markings

Patches of fur on a horse's or pony's body that are different in colour to their coat are called markings. They are often white and are most common on the face and legs. Patches of white fur on other parts of an animal's body are called flesh marks.

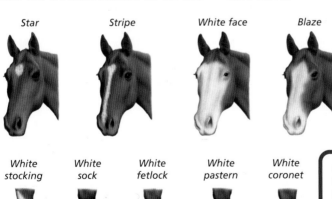

| *Star* | *Stripe* | *White face* | *Blaze* | *Snip* |

| *White stocking* | *White sock* | *White fetlock* | *White pastern* | *White coronet* |

An **eel stripe** is a line of dark fur growing along a horse's or pony's spine. Eel stripes are common in primitive breeds and dun-coloured animals.

CARING FOR A HORSE OR PONY

Looking after a horse or pony is a big responsibility. It takes time, money, patience, hard work – and lots of love and care.

HORSE AND PONY HOMES

Horses and ponies are usually kept in livery yards, or stables. These are places often run as businesses by riding schools, where lots of horses and ponies can be cared for together. The animals are looked after by experienced professionals. A stable should be kept clean, with plenty of light and fresh air. All horses and ponies need shelter, especially during the winter. They also benefit from having open spaces to run around and exercise.

Hay

Mare and foal

Carrots

Dirty bedding

Mucking out

The work involved in keeping stables clean and comfortable is called stable management. One of the most important parts of this work is mucking out – removing droppings and wet bedding.

This has to be done every day. After the old bedding and dirt has been removed the floor is left to dry, if possible, before clean wood shavings and straw are laid down.

Staying safe

Putting a horse or pony in a field, or paddock, is called 'turning out'. Fields need to be checked regularly and dangerous plants removed. Ragwort, foxgloves, laburnum and acorns are just a few plants that can cause a horse or pony health problems. These plants have to be dug out or cut back from a field's edges.

Droppings also need to be removed from fields. This helps to prevent worms, which live inside horses' and ponies' bodies and spread through droppings.

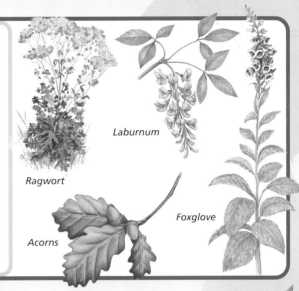

Laburnum

Ragwort

Foxglove

Acorns

Farriers

People who replace horses' and ponies' shoes are called farriers. They trim the hooves, which doesn't hurt the animal, to make sure the shoes fit properly. Horses and ponies need to have the underside of their hooves checked regularly, and stones should be removed with a hoof pick.

Farrier

STAYING HEALTHY

To stay fit and healthy, horses and ponies need to be kept well-fed and watered. They also need to be kept clean and groomed. Occasionally, a vet will need to tend to medical problems.

FEEDING

In the wild, equids graze slowly for most of the day, so their bodies are not used to coping with a lot of food at one time.

Horses and ponies should eat small amounts several times a day. Animals that live in fields need less feeding than stabled animals because they can graze on grass. Working horses and ponies need to eat more as they burn up lots of energy.

The diet of horses and ponies is mostly made up of bulk feed – grass and hay.

Hard feed is used to add extra nutrients and goodness. Oats, bran, maize, sugar beet, barley, pony nuts and coarse mix are all examples of hard feed. These types of food are usually mixed up with chaff, which is chopped hay or straw.

Pony nuts   Barley   Oats

Swedes, carrots, apples and turnips can all be given as treats, but not too many at a time.

▶ Horses and ponies must always have fresh food to eat, and access to clean water.

Hay

Water

Watering

Horses and ponies should have access to drinking water at all times – except straight after feeding. If they drink straight after a feed they can suffer from colic, which causes abdominal pain. If an animal is suffering with colic, it will often roll on the ground and may lay down and get up a lot.

Grooming

Keeping a horse or pony clean and groomed helps to prevent illness and parasites. It also brings the animal and its owner closer together, helping them to bond and trust each other.

Horses and ponies should only be washed occasionally, if they get very dirty. The corners of their eyes, muzzle and nostrils can be cleaned daily with a damp sponge.

Grooming is usually enough to keep a horse or pony clean. People who care for them are taught the best ways to groom and the best equipment to use. A grooming kit includes a dandy brush for removing dry mud, a body brush for removing grease and dust, a hoof pick and a mane comb.

Vets

While a careful owner can do a great deal to keep their animal in good health, a vet's services are essential when problems arise, such as swollen and sore hooves or lameness. Vets can also deal with common pests and parasites that may distress an animal, such as worms, mites and bot-flies.

TACK

Riding a horse or pony requires special equipment, called **tack.** It includes a saddle, bridle and stirrups. Most tack is made from leather and metal. Putting on tack to prepare a horse or pony to be ridden is called tacking up.

Bridles and bits

The equipment that is fitted on a horse's or pony's head is called the bridle, and it helps the rider to control the animal. Bridles are made of leather so they are comfortable for the animal to wear. A stainless steel mouthpiece, called a bit, is attached to the bridle and sits in the horse's or pony's mouth. It is controlled by gentle use of the reins.

Saddles

A saddle is a special seat made of leather. It is held in place by a strap called a girth. The saddle helps the horse and the rider stay comfortable and safe. There are different saddles for different activities, such as racing or showjumping.

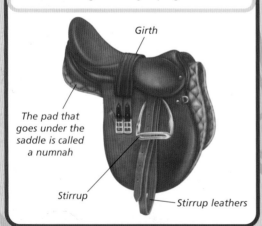

Girth

The pad that goes under the saddle is called a numnah

Stirrup

Stirrup leathers

Stirrups

The footrests that support a rider's feet are called stirrups. They help the rider to control the horse or pony. Riders usually wear shoes or boots with heels to stop their feet getting trapped in the stirrups.

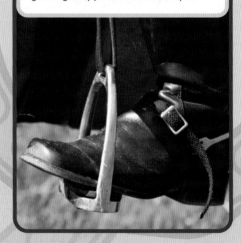

Headcollars

Headcollars are made of leather or webbing and have straps that can be adjusted to make sure they fit well. A rope can be attached to a headcollar to lead or tie up a horse or pony.

Hackamores

A hackamore is a type of bridle that does not use a bit for control. Instead, a heavy noseband is used to train the horse or pony. Hackamores are often used in western riding in the USA.

Rugs and blankets

In cold weather, horses and ponies may need to be gently covered with rugs or blankets to keep them warm. They are placed over their backs and strapped into place. Sweat rugs are made of mesh and help horses to cool down after exercise, while waterproof rugs, called New Zealand rugs, keep them dry outdoors. Summer sheets keep them clean during journeys and at shows.

WORK AND PLAY

Spending time with horses and ponies and riding them can be enormous fun, but it takes time and patience to learn how to control them. Horses and ponies can be unpredictable and dangerous, so it is important to treat these large animals with respect.

Meeting and greeting

Horses and ponies are sensitive to people's moods, so a nervous or anxious person can make them feel unsettled. The best way to approach a horse or pony is slowly, with your hand held out, palm-side down and with your fingers curled. Gently talking to the animal and letting it sniff you and look at you are good ways to help it relax.

Mounting and dismounting

Getting up into the saddle is called mounting and getting off is called dismounting. Horses and ponies are always mounted from their left side.

The rider holds the reins and places their left hand on the animal's withers, while putting their left foot in the stirrup and right hand on the back of the saddle. A quick spring up, swinging the right leg over the horse's back, is all it takes to get into position.

To safely dismount, the rider takes both feet out of the stirrups. Then leaning forward and swinging their right leg over the animal's back, both feet can drop to the floor at the same time.

Controlling a pony

Riders control their horse or pony using signals that the animal has been trained to follow. The signals tell the horse or pony whether to speed up, slow down or stop. They also direct the horse or pony to go left or right.

Riders use their legs, feet, hands and seat to send directions to their horse or pony, as well as giving instructions using their voice. Some riders also use whips to give their horse or pony a tap, but only if they ignore other signals.

Gaits

Horses and ponies have four main gaits, or speeds. Walk is the slowest and gallop is the fastest. In canter and gallop there are moments when all four feet are in the air – this is called the suspension.

◀ *Walk has a four-beat rhythm. The horse places its left foreleg forwards, then its right hind leg, followed by its right foreleg and then its left hind leg.*

▶ *Trot is the next fastest gait and it has a two-beat rhythm. Two legs (for example the left foreleg and the right hind leg) touch the ground at the same time, while the other legs are in the air.*

◀ *Canter has a three-beat rhythm. There is a moment when all four feet are off the ground.*

▶ *Gallop is the fastest gait. It is similar to canter but it is faster and with longer strides. It has a four-beat rhythm.*

HOW TO USE THIS BOOK

U se this guide to help you find your way around this book. There's information about each breed, including vital statistics, amazing facts and a photo file. You can add your own notes and pictures in the write-in area.

Photo file
Photos show each breed in its natural habitat or working environment and help to highlight particular characteristics.

Fact file
Provides essential facts and information.

Super fact
Find out amazing information about every breed.

Group colours
These tell you which group a particular breed is in.
Orange = Hotblood horses
Purple = Warmblood horses
Blue = Coldblood horses
Green = Ponies

You can find the breeds in their groups on the poster.

Write-in area
Draw pictures, stick in photos and add notes, ideas and thoughts about the horses and ponies you see.

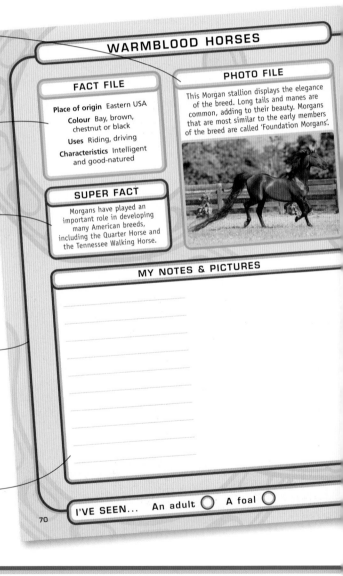

WARMBLOOD HORSES

FACT FILE

Place of origin Eastern USA
Colour Bay, brown, chestnut or black
Uses Riding, driving
Characteristics Intelligent and good-natured

SUPER FACT

Morgans have played an important role in developing many American breeds, including the Quarter Horse and the Tennessee Walking Horse.

PHOTO FILE

This Morgan stallion displays the elegance of the breed. Long tails and manes are common, adding to their beauty. Morgans that are most similar to the early members of the breed are called 'Foundation Morgans'.

MY NOTES & PICTURES

I'VE SEEN... An adult ◯ A foal ◯

70

Each breed in this book is compared against a silhouette of a person. This will help you to understand how big or small it actually is.

An average person is about 1.8 m in height

MORGAN

The Morgan – possibly the first breed to be developed in America – descended from a stallion called Justin Morgan. This original Morgan is thought to have been a mix of Arab and Thoroughbred and was named after its owner. The breed became famous for its abilities to work hard on the farm as well as for competing successfully in shows. Morgans are known for their gentle, affectionate natures.

HEIGHT
14.1–15.1 hh

Text
Every right-hand page introduces you to a different breed.

Arab-like face

Arched neck holds head high

Rounded hindquarters

Tail can be very long

Tapering muzzle

Long, sloping shoulders

Long, compact body

Neat hooves

Main photo
Beautiful photographs are labelled to help you identify key characteristics.

IN A... Field ◯ Stable ◯ Show ◯ TV/Film ◯ 71

Keep a record
Tick the circles to show what you've seen and where you've seen it.

HOTBLOOD HORSES

FACT FILE

Place of origin Turkmenistan

Colour Metallic gold, bay, grey, chestnut, black or palomino

Uses Long-distance racing, showjumping, dressage

Characteristics Courageous and strong

SUPER FACT

In 1935, the strength and power of Akhal-Tekes was proved when Turkish horsemen rode a group for 4000 kilometres in just 84 days.

PHOTO FILE

Akhal-Tekes are most distinctive for their unusual lustrous, metallic colouring. Even dark-coloured Akhal-Tekes have a glossy sheen to their coats. The most prized colour of the breed is golden.

MY NOTES & PICTURES

I'VE SEEN... An adult   A foal

AKHAL-TEKE

Known for its beautiful, metallic coat, the classic Akhal-Teke is a hotblood that is both resilient and powerful. These horses were originally bred in the deserts of Turkmenistan, Central Asia, and they cope well with the intense heat of the desert and the scarcity of food and water. Akhal-Tekes are naturally athletic. Today, they are ridden in long-distance races, as well as dressage and showjumping.

HEIGHT
14.3–16 hh

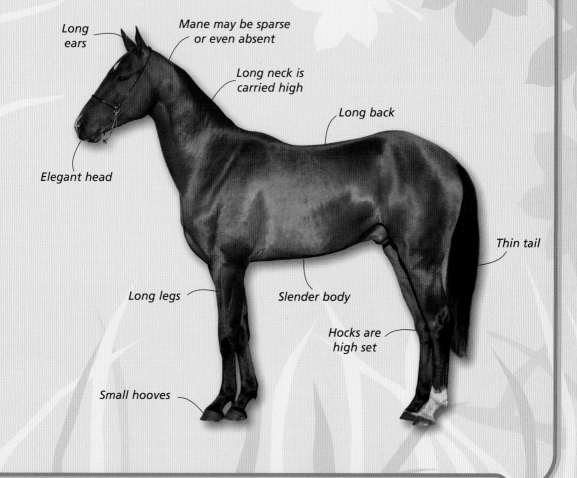

Long ears

Mane may be sparse or even absent

Long neck is carried high

Long back

Elegant head

Thin tail

Long legs

Slender body

Hocks are high set

Small hooves

WARMBLOOD HORSES

FACT FILE

Place of origin Southern Spain

Colour Mostly grey. Bay and black are rare

Uses Riding, dressage, driving

Characteristics Agile and calm

SUPER FACT

Andalucians are one of the oldest breeds. They originate from ancient horses that are depicted in prehistoric cave paintings, in Spain, interacting with people.

PHOTO FILE

Thousands of visitors flock to the Spanish town of Jerez every year to enjoy the annual horse fair. At this traditional event the Andalucian horses are decorated to look their best.

MY NOTES & PICTURES

I'VE SEEN... An adult A foal

ANDALUCIAN

This breed is known for its elegant looks and long mane. Andalucians are intelligent warmbloods – they learn quickly and respond well to riders. This breed descended from wild Spanish horses and has been used to develop most modern horse breeds, including Lipizzaners, Connemaras and Welsh Cobs. In the 1700s, the breed nearly died out following a period of famine and plague in Europe.

HEIGHT
15–16.2 hh

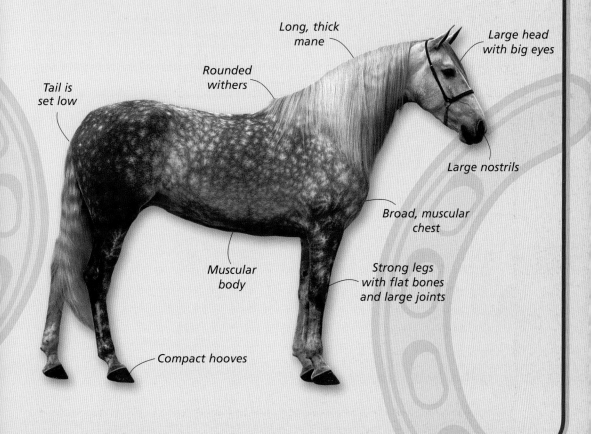

Long, thick mane

Large head with big eyes

Rounded withers

Tail is set low

Large nostrils

Broad, muscular chest

Muscular body

Strong legs with flat bones and large joints

Compact hooves

IN A... Field ◯   Stable ◯   Show ◯   TV/Film ◯

HOTBLOOD HORSES

FACT FILE

Place of origin England

Colour Chestnut, brown, bay or grey

Uses Riding, showjumping, dressage, long-distance racing

Characteristics Intelligent and fast

SUPER FACT

Anglo-Arabs are popular horses for endurance racing. During races they may cover distances of up to 80 kilometres a day.

PHOTO FILE

Anglo-Arabs are popular with championship riders and compete at high level events, including the Olympic Games. Successful riders and their horses develop strong bonds and often work together for many years.

MY NOTES & PICTURES

I'VE SEEN... An adult A foal

ANGLO-ARAB

The Anglo-Arab is a cross between the Arab, giving it elegance and strength, and the Thoroughbred, giving it speed and intelligence. Anglo-Arabs are especially popular in France where they are bred for use in general riding and competitions. Although they are slightly smaller than Thoroughbreds, Anglo-Arabs have long legs, making them ideal for showjumping. They are also often used in the game of polo.

HEIGHT
15.2–16.3 hh

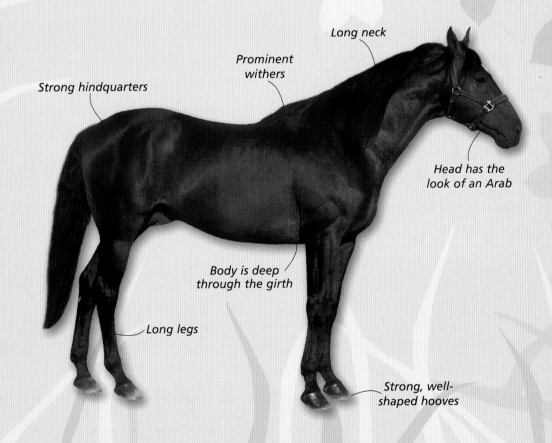

Long neck

Prominent withers

Strong hindquarters

Head has the look of an Arab

Body is deep through the girth

Long legs

Strong, well-shaped hooves

WARMBLOOD HORSES

FACT FILE

Place of origin Washington, USA

Colour Spotted coats of varying colours

Uses Riding, showjumping, showing, dressage

Characteristics Athletic and versatile

SUPER FACT

In some countries, the Appaloosa is recognized as a colour variety, but not a pure breed. In the USA they are a registered breed.

PHOTO FILE

The Appaloosa leopard pattern is white with coloured spots. Dark fur with white spots is called the snowflake pattern. Cave paintings in France suggest that spotted horses have been around for at least 18,000 years.

MY NOTES & PICTURES

I'VE SEEN...   An adult ◯   A foal ◯

APPALOOSA

Appaloosas have been bred from Quarter Horses, making this breed particularly strong and good-natured. In the 1700s, American Indians developed the breed by mixing their own native horses with spotted Spanish horses that were introduced to America in the 1600s. The American Indians favoured spots and patches of colour, which led to a variety of coat patterns. Appaloosas were kept as work horses but now they are developed for showjumping and dressage.

HEIGHT
14.2–15.2 hh

White ring visible around the iris

Short, thin mane and tail

This colouring is known as spotted blanket – the body is coloured but the back and hindquarters are white with coloured spots

Mottled skin around the nose

Sloping shoulders

Hooves are often stripy

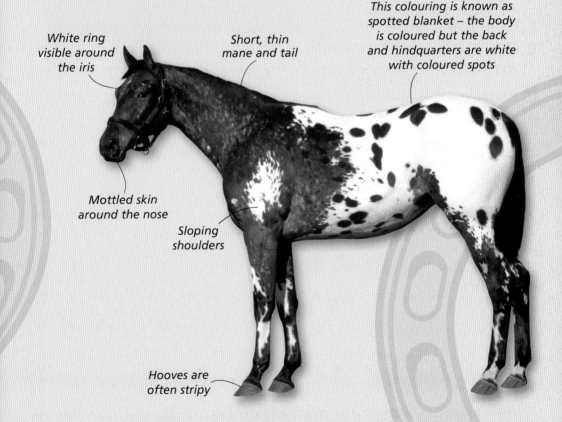

HOTBLOOD HORSES

FACT FILE

Place of origin Arabian peninsula

Colour Grey, chestnut or bay. Brown or black is rare

Uses Riding, racing, showing

Characteristics Intelligent and high-spirited

PHOTO FILE

Arabs were once raced through the deserts of the Middle East. Today, they are raced along racetracks at speed. They are also particularly favoured in long races where their endurance is valued.

SUPER FACT

The first Arabian horses were probably bred at least 1400 years ago. Most types of modern horse have Arabian bloodlines.

MY NOTES & PICTURES

I'VE SEEN... An adult ◯ A foal ◯

ARAB

Arabian horses are one of the oldest known breeds. Arabs are beautiful, clever and gentle, and are especially valued for the their great speed and stamina. These horses have unusually short bodies because their spines have fewer bones than in other breeds. Arabs are high-spirited, but they handle well, making them popular with riders. Because of their genetic purity, Arabs have been used for centuries to improve and refine many other breeds around the world.

HEIGHT
14.2–15 hh +

Small head with large eyes

Silky mane and tail

Tail is carried high

Short back

Small muzzle

The Mitbah is the name given to the angle at which the head meets the neck in Arabs

Body is deep through the girth

Flat knees

HOTBLOOD HORSES

FACT FILE

Place of origin North Africa

Colour Bay, brown or grey

Uses Riding, racing

Characteristics Strong and tough

SUPER FACT

The Abaco Barb is an endangered strain of the breed that lives on the island of Abaco in the Bahamas. The horses were shipwrecked there 500 years ago.

PHOTO FILE

For centuries, Berber warriors of North Africa have ridden Barbs in battle. These horses are courageous, agile and responsive to the slightest movement of the reins, making them ideal cavalry horses in close combat.

MY NOTES & PICTURES

I'VE SEEN... An adult   A foal

BARB

No one knows exactly when the first Barb horses appeared, but it is thought they developed after North African wild horses bred with Arabs or Akhal-Tekes. Barbs are extremely strong and have good stamina, although they lack the elegance of other hotbloods. The Barb is one of the world's most ancient breeds. It has been used to breed many other types of modern horse, but their numbers as a pure breed are falling.

HEIGHT
13.3–14.1 hh

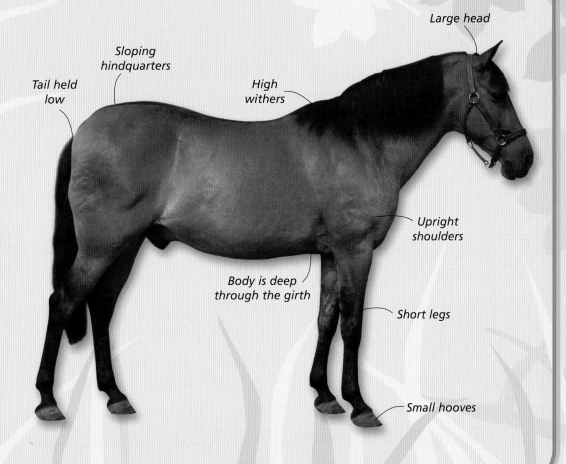

Large head

Sloping hindquarters

Tail held low

High withers

Upright shoulders

Body is deep through the girth

Short legs

Small hooves

COLDBLOOD HORSES

FACT FILE

Place of origin France

Colour Usually grey. Other colours are rare

Uses Farm work, pulling

Characteristics Calm and strong

SUPER FACT

Boulonnais' are usually grey, but breeders are now trying to introduce black back into the breed. Black Boulonnais horses were common 200 years ago.

PHOTO FILE

Draught horses such as the Boulonnais are used for pulling heavy loads, especially farm equipment. Before tractors were invented, farmers relied on draught horses for jobs such as ploughing.

MY NOTES & PICTURES

I'VE SEEN... An adult ◯ A foal ◯

BOULONNAIS

According to legend, these sturdy coldbloods were bred from horses brought to France by Roman general Julius Caesar when he was preparing to invade Britain in the first century BC. Boulonnais horses are strong, but they also have elegance from their Arab ancestors. In the 17th century, they were used to carry loads of fish over 300 kilometres from the coast to markets in Paris. These popular draught horses are still bred in parts of northern France.

HEIGHT
15.3–16.3 hh

Small ears

Elegant head

Muscular, curved neck

Fine coat

Straight back

Well-opened nostrils

Wide chest

Powerful shoulders

Legs have less feather than in other draught breeds

WARMBLOOD HORSES

FACT FILE

Place of origin Camargue
region of France

Colour Grey

Uses Cattle herding

Characteristics Tough
and courageous

PHOTO FILE

These horses are known as the 'wild white horses of the sea' as they are often pictured galloping through wetlands of the river Rhône. In the wild, Camargues prefer to live in a group, or herd.

SUPER FACT

Camargues are black or brown at birth. White hairs gradually grow through their dark coats and by their fourth year, Camargues are completely white, or grey.

MY NOTES & PICTURES

I'VE SEEN...   An adult ◯   A foal ◯

CAMARGUE

Camargues are now bred as riding horses, but for a long time they lived as a wild breed in southern France. Surviving in the wild meant that these small horses developed toughness and strength. Despite their size, Camargues can carry the weight of an adult with ease, and are used to round up wild bulls for bullfights. They were tamed by the Romans and were probably bred with European horses to develop other modern types, such as the Criollo of Argentina.

HEIGHT
13–14 hh

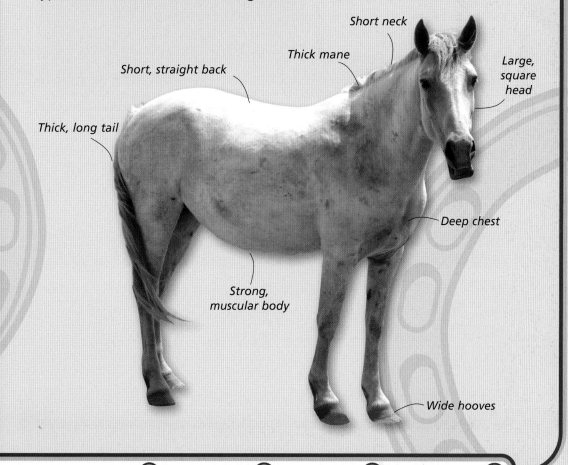

Short neck

Thick mane

Short, straight back

Thick, long tail

Large, square head

Deep chest

Strong, muscular body

Wide hooves

IN A... Field ◯   Stable ◯   Show ◯   TV/Film ◯

PONIES

FACT FILE

Place of origin Iran

Colour All, but bay or chestnut
are common

Uses Riding, showing, pulling

Characteristics Fast
and strong

SUPER FACT

This breed was rediscovered in
the last century. Caspians are
now being carefully bred in
several countries to ensure
their survival.

PHOTO FILE

This ancient pony breed has a long history
of driving and pulling and is still worked
in harness today. Caspian ponies grow
unusually quickly and reach adult height
by the end of their first six months.

MY NOTES & PICTURES

I'VE SEEN...   An adult   A foal

CASPIAN

The little Caspian is often regarded as one of the oldest breeds of horse or pony, and may even be an ancestor of the great Arab. There is evidence that these ponies have lived near the Caspian Sea, in what is now Iran, since prehistoric times. Carvings and friezes from the Middle East dating to 3000 BC depict these small ponies. Caspian ponies are used to pull carts and they also make good riding ponies for children.

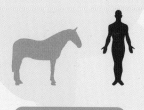

HEIGHT
10–12 hh

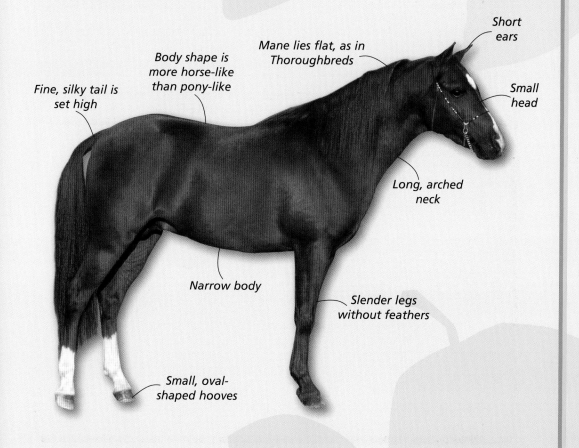

Short ears

Mane lies flat, as in Thoroughbreds

Body shape is more horse-like than pony-like

Fine, silky tail is set high

Small head

Long, arched neck

Narrow body

Slender legs without feathers

Small, oval-shaped hooves

WARMBLOOD HORSES

FACT FILE

Place of origin England

Colour Bay

Uses Riding, driving

Characteristics Intelligent and bold

SUPER FACT

The Cleveland Bay is the rarest and oldest of British breeds. It is used to cross with other breeds, so pure breeds have almost disappeared.

PHOTO FILE

His Royal Highness Prince Philip enjoys horse driving and uses teams of horses that often include Cleveland Bays. Horses are selected for a team according to their size, strength and temperament.

MY NOTES & PICTURES

I'VE SEEN...　An adult 　A foal

CLEVELAND BAY

Cleveland Bays have gentle natures. They have been bred in Britain since the Middle Ages, mostly in northern England. Much admired for their elegant step and good nature, these warmbloods were popular carriage horses and are still used to pull royal carriages today. Cleveland Bays were used during World War I (1914–1918) to pull guns and were able to work for many hours before tiring.

HEIGHT
15.3–16.2 hh

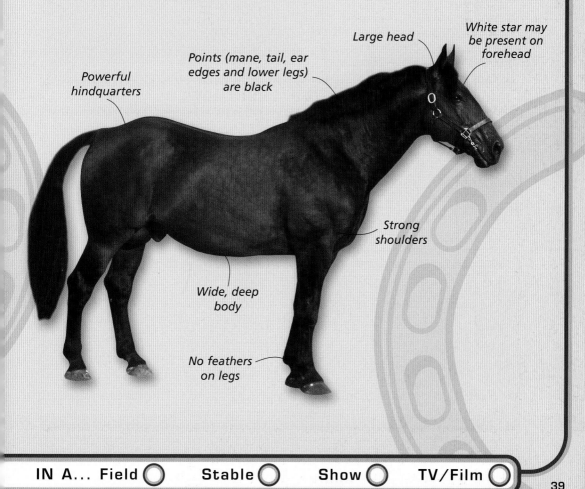

Large head

White star may be present on forehead

Points (mane, tail, ear edges and lower legs) are black

Powerful hindquarters

Strong shoulders

Wide, deep body

No feathers on legs

COLDBLOOD HORSES

FACT FILE

Place of origin Scotland

Colour Brown, bay, black or roan

Uses Showing, pulling

Characteristics Quiet and strong

SUPER FACT

Before a Clydesdale foal can be registered as a pedigree, a sample of its hair is sent for testing to prove its parents were both Clydesdales.

PHOTO FILE

Clydesdales and other draught horses need special tack for pulling farm equipment. These horses are wearing large head collars made of leather and stuffed with straw. They are comfortable for the horses to wear.

MY NOTES & PICTURES

I'VE SEEN... An adult A foal

CLYDESDALE

Clydesdales have been bred in Scotland since the 17th century. Native horses were crossed with larger stallions brought over from Europe, to develop this heavier, stronger breed. Clydesdales were originally used to pull ploughs and many were sent to Australia and New Zealand in the 1800s to work on farms. Many horses were also transported to France during World War I (1914 –1918) where they were used for pulling heavy guns and transporting supplies. As tractors became more common, Clydesdale numbers dropped dramatically.

HEIGHT
17 hh

Broad forehead

Head has straight profile

High withers

Muscular hindquarters

Bay and brown, with white markings are most common

Body is deep through the girth

Large hooves

Silky feathers around feet

PONIES

FACT FILE

Place of origin Ireland

Colour Grey, dun, chestnut, bay, roan, brown or black

Uses Riding, eventing

Characteristics Friendly and intelligent

SUPER FACT

In 1926, the first Connemara pony stud book was published by a group of local Connemara men, who formed themselves into the Connemara Pony Breeders Society.

PHOTO FILE

The most famous show for these ponies is the Annual Clifden Connemara Pony Show in Ireland. Ponies are shown in in-hand and ridden classes and both pony and rider are judged on appearance and behaviour.

MY NOTES & PICTURES

I'VE SEEN...   An adult   A foal

CONNEMARA

These sturdy, yet gentle ponies are popular with both children and adults. Connemaras have lived in Ireland for hundreds of years and are thought to have a mixture of Spanish, Barb, Arab, Thoroughbred and Welsh Cob blood. Connemaras cope with the harsh weather conditions of the moors and are known for their hardiness. They have good jumping ability and are often used in hunts and shown in competitions. Although Connemaras were originally dun, they now appear in many colours.

HEIGHT
12.2–14.2 hh

Small ears

Well-arched neck

Powerful hindquarters

Long, thick tail

Short back

Compact head

Sloping shoulders

Short, strong legs

PONIES

FACT FILE

Place of origin England

Colour Bay, brown, black, chestnut, roan or grey

Uses Riding

Characteristics Strong and resilient

SUPER FACT

Dartmoor ponies were bred at a prison in the 1900s, up until 1960. The guards used them to transport prisoners to and from jail.

PHOTO FILE

Wild ponies living on Dartmoor help to maintain this important habitat for other animals and plants. By grazing on the moor, the ponies keep the trees and prickly gorse bushes under control.

MY NOTES & PICTURES

I'VE SEEN...   An adult ◯   A foal ◯
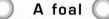

DARTMOOR

Dartmoor ponies have survived on the **moors of southwest England for at least 1000 years.** These animals are not pure-bred, but have been crossed with Thoroughbreds and Arabs to improve the breed. Dartmoor ponies are also bred for use as childrens' riding ponies. They have gentle natures, making them suitable for children who are learning to ride and care for a pony.

HEIGHT
11.1–12.2 hh

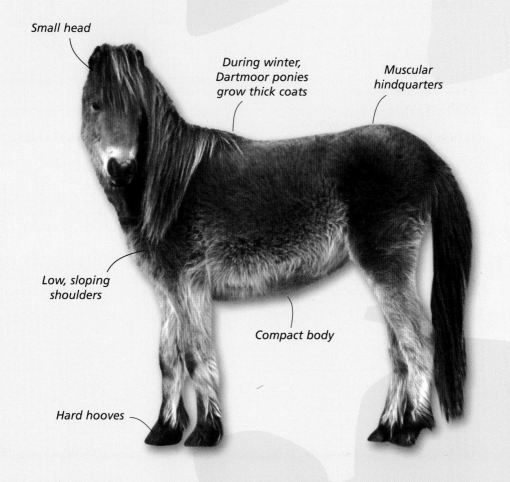

Small head

During winter, Dartmoor ponies grow thick coats

Muscular hindquarters

Low, sloping shoulders

Compact body

Hard hooves

IN A... Field ◯　　　Stable ◯　　　Show ◯　　　TV/Film ◯

COLDBLOOD HORSES

FACT FILE

Place of origin Holland

Colour Chestnut, roan, bay, black or grey

Uses Showing, pulling

Characteristics Powerful and calm

SUPER FACT

The long-lived Dutch Draught is famous for its ability to work in tough environments for long stretches of time.

PHOTO FILE

The massive legs of the Dutch Draught are obvious, despite carrying a lot of feather around its hooves. Since the mechanization of farm equipment, they are more often seen in shows, pulling carts and heavy loads.

MY NOTES & PICTURES

I'VE SEEN... An adult A foal

DUTCH DRAUGHT

The heavy clay soils in parts of Holland made pulling ploughs tough work for all but the strongest horses. To solve this problem, farmers bred Dutch Draught horses, which are the heaviest of all coldbloods. They are strong and sure-footed, and are known for their quiet, patient temperaments. Despite their great size, Dutch Draughts can move in a sprightly, energetic way. It is rare for these coldbloods to work on farms today, but they are often seen in show rings, pulling carriages.

HEIGHT
16–17 hh

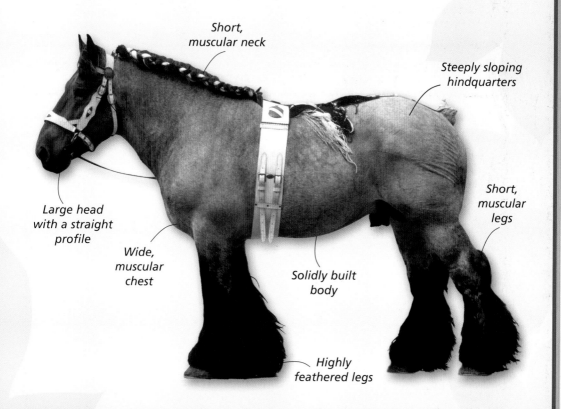

Short, muscular neck

Steeply sloping hindquarters

Large head with a straight profile

Short, muscular legs

Wide, muscular chest

Solidly built body

Highly feathered legs

WARMBLOOD HORSES

FACT FILE

Place of origin The Netherlands

Colour Black, brown, bay, chestnut or grey

Uses Showjumping, dressage

Characteristics Tough and long-lived

SUPER FACT

Dutch Warmbloods are extremely fit and strong and resistant to health problems. This is due to the careful way they are bred.

PHOTO FILE

Dutch Warmbloods are successful in showjumping events. Riders and their mounts have to clear a round of jumps against the clock. Penalties are given for knocking down fences and exceeding the time limit.

MY NOTES & PICTURES

I'VE SEEN... An adult ◯ A foal ◯

DUTCH WARMBLOOD

The Dutch Warmblood is one of the world's youngest breeds. It was developed in the 1960s by breeding Dutch horses with English Thoroughbreds. They have been bred for competitions such as dressage and showjumping, and are one of the most successful competition breeds ever produced. Only horses that are quick to obey instruction and easy to handle are allowed to breed. Most have coats of a solid colour, although white markings on the legs and head are common.

HEIGHT
15.3–16.3 hh

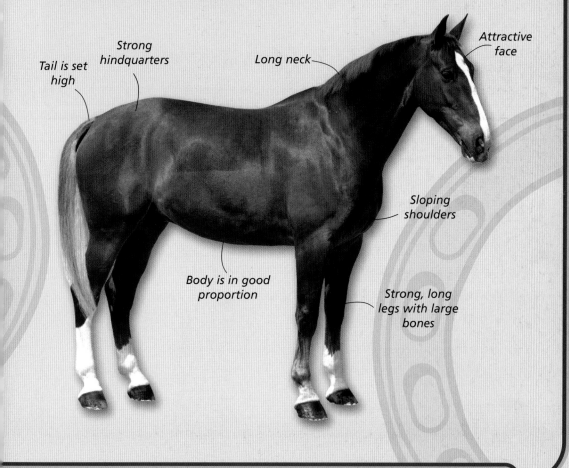

Tail is set high

Strong hindquarters

Long neck

Attractive face

Sloping shoulders

Body is in good proportion

Strong, long legs with large bones

PONIES

FACT FILE

Place of origin England

Colour Bay, brown or dun

Uses Riding

Characteristics Tough and hard-working

SUPER FACT

In the 1940s, Exmoor ponies nearly became extinct. Their numbers have increased since, but they are currently listed as an 'endangered' breed of pony.

PHOTO FILE

Like Dartmoors, Exmoor ponies grow thick fur and manes in the winter. During spring and summer, Exmoors graze on nutritious grasses. During winter, as food becomes scarce, they feed on tough gorse bushes.

MY NOTES & PICTURES

I'VE SEEN...   An adult   A foal ◯

EXMOOR

Exmoor ponies may be small – standing around 12 hands high – but they are tough and resilient. Their strength and hardiness comes from the environment they have to survive. They are one of the world's oldest breeds – dating back to the Ice Age – and still survive as a free-living, wild herd on Exmoor. Tame Exmoors are also bred as riding ponies and are often used by groups of disabled children due to their gentle and reliable natures.

HEIGHT
12.2–12.3 hh

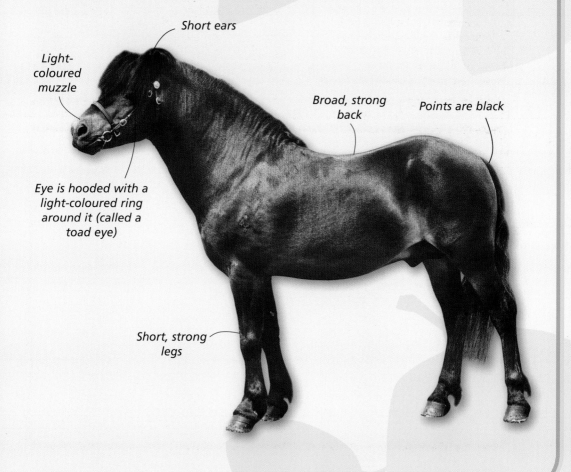

Short ears

Light-coloured muzzle

Eye is hooded with a light-coloured ring around it (called a toad eye)

Broad, strong back

Points are black

Short, strong legs

PONIES

FACT FILE

Place of origin Argentina

Colour Any

Uses Showing

Characteristics Friendly and intelligent

SUPER FACT

Falabellas were first developed by the Falabella family of Argentina, by breeding a small Shetland pony with a small Thoroughbred horse.

PHOTO FILE

Falabellas have 12- to 13-month-long pregancies – two months longer than other breeds. Foals stand around 20 cm tall at birth and they reach their adult height by the end of their second year.

MY NOTES & PICTURES

I'VE SEEN... An adult A foal ⃝

FALABELLA

The tiny Falabella is one of the world's smallest and rarest breeds. They are often called miniature horses because they have the proportions of a horse. Falabellas are the result of selective breeding. Over many years, only the smallest animals were chosen to breed, which encouraged smaller and smaller foals. However they are not very strong and can only be ridden by very young children.

HEIGHT
7–8.2 hh

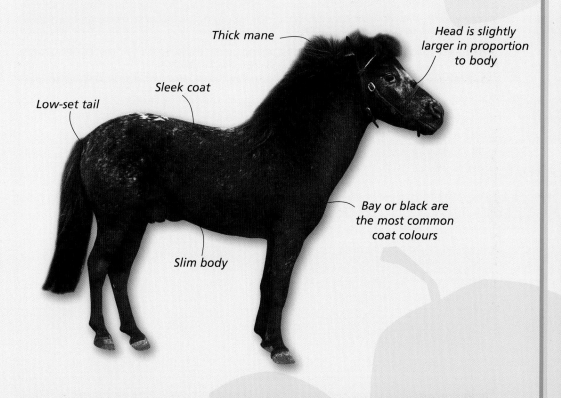

Thick mane

Head is slightly larger in proportion to body

Sleek coat

Low-set tail

Bay or black are the most common coat colours

Slim body

IN A... Field ○   Stable ○   Show ○   TV/Film ○

PONIES

FACT FILE

Place of origin England

Colour Dark brown or black

Uses Riding, driving, trekking

Characteristics Hard-working and strong

SUPER FACT

Fell pony numbers were declining 50 years ago. Now, these ponies are one of Britain's most popular native breeds, although their numbers are still less than 6000.

PHOTO FILE

The Fell Pony Society was set up in 1916 to ensure the future of the breed, and HRH Queen Elizabeth II is the patron. As below, HRH Prince Philip often competes in driving events with teams of Fell ponies.

MY NOTES & PICTURES

I'VE SEEN... An adult A foal ◯

FELL

Fell ponies are one of the oldest native breeds and have played an important role in British history. They are known for their sure-footedness, which meant they were perfect for carrying loads on awkward routes. Because of this, they were often used by smugglers in Britain during the 17th and 18th centuries. They were also used on farms, to carry loads from mines and for riding. Today, they are popular as family riding ponies, and for driving, showing, trekking and hunting.

HEIGHT
13–14 hh

Small ears

Long, full mane and tail

Square hindquarters

Large nostrils

Small, well-shaped head

Fine feather around heels

White markings are rare, but may occur as a star behind the fetlock

Well-formed hooves with slight blue colour

PONIES

FACT FILE

Place of origin Norway

Colour Dun

Uses Riding

Characteristics Calm and intelligent

SUPER FACT

Although Fjords are pony-sized, they are often referred to as horses. Fjords rarely grow taller than 14.2 hands high – the top height limit for ponies.

PHOTO FILE

Wild Fjord ponies cope well in cold conditions because they grow thick coats in winter. This is one of the ways their ancestors adapted to survive in Norway for hundreds of years.

MY NOTES & PICTURES

I'VE SEEN... An adult ◯ A foal ◯

FJORD

Fjord ponies are an ancient breed that bear some primitive characteristics, also seen in Przewalski's Horses. These ponies get their name from the fjord regions in Norway where they originate from and they have been ridden and worked by people since around 4000 years ago. Fjords have developed without cross-breeding, making them one of the purest breeds. They are known for their strength and have been used to pull loads and ploughs. Today they are used as riding ponies, especially for children.

HEIGHT
13–14.2 hh

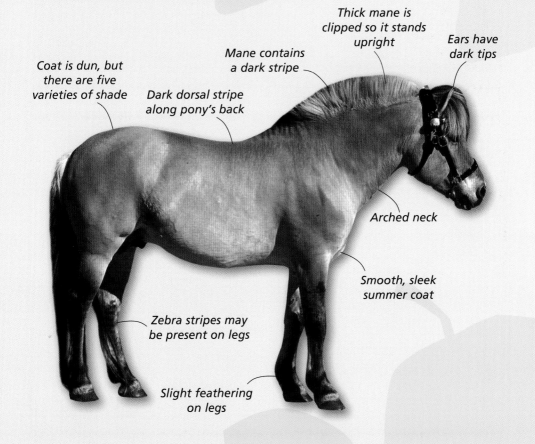

Coat is dun, but there are five varieties of shade

Dark dorsal stripe along pony's back

Mane contains a dark stripe

Thick mane is clipped so it stands upright

Ears have dark tips

Arched neck

Smooth, sleek summer coat

Zebra stripes may be present on legs

Slight feathering on legs

WARMBLOOD HORSES

FACT FILE

Place of origin England

Colour Can be any colour, but mostly bay, chestnut or black

Uses Driving

Characteristics Sprightly and energetic

SUPER FACT

Hackneys have been developed as ponies as well as horses. They are one of few breeds that recognize both horse and pony sizes.

PHOTO FILE

Hackney Horses are often seen in shows in-harness pulling carriages or traps. These horses are best known for their elegant, floating trotting action – they raise their knees high and pause in between each stride.

MY NOTES & PICTURES

I'VE SEEN... An adult ◯ A foal ◯

HACKNEY HORSE

Hackneys are probably the world's best-known carriage horses. They were bred in England in the 18th and 19th centuries from the Yorkshire Roadster and the Norfolk Trotter, and were then crossed with Thoroughbreds. Hackney Horses are strong and have an elegant high step. Before cars, Hackneys were used to pull carriages and were favoured for their grace. As a Hackney Horse moves, it throws its forelegs forward, keeping its knees high.

HEIGHT
14.2–16.2 hh

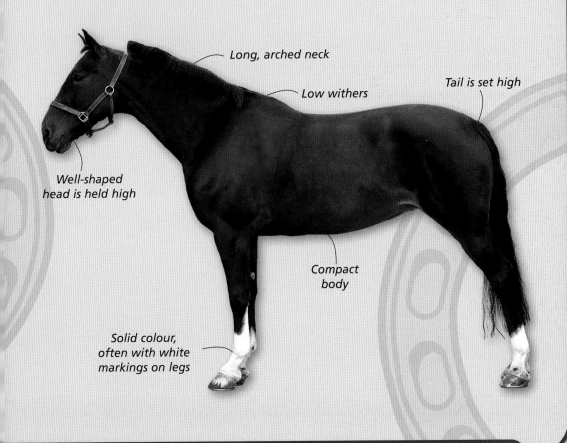

Long, arched neck

Low withers

Tail is set high

Well-shaped
head is held high

Compact
body

Solid colour,
often with white
markings on legs

PONIES

FACT FILE

Place of origin Austria

Colour Chestnut, with flaxen or white mane and tail

Uses Driving, riding, trekking

Characteristics Long-lived and hardy

SUPER FACT

Austrian Haflingers are branded on their left thigh with the letter 'H' and a symbol of the edelweiss – Austria's national flower.

PHOTO FILE

Haflingers are descended from mountain ponies. Some people consider them to be small horses rather than ponies because of their body shape. They have Arab ancestors too, which explains their well-shaped heads.

MY NOTES & PICTURES

I'VE SEEN...   An adult   A foal

HAFLINGER

Known as 'golden horses', Haflingers are pretty ponies with chestnut coats and white manes. These Austrian ponies were bred from native animals that were used on farms in the mountains. The modern breed was established in the 19th century from a stallion called Folie 249. Today, all Haflingers trace their ancestry back to this stallion. Haflingers have been transported around the world, becoming an international breed. They are friendly, calm ponies, making them popular with families.

HEIGHT
13–14.2 hh

Chestnut coat

White or flaxen (pale yellow) mane and tail

Large, expressive eyes

Well-shaped head

Stocky body

Strong legs and feet

PONIES

FACT FILE

Place of origin Scotland

Colour Brown, black, dun or grey

Uses Riding, driving, trekking

Characteristics Hard-working and strong

SUPER FACT

There were once three types of Highland pony. Ponies from the Scottish islands were smaller than those from the mainland. Today there is just one breed.

PHOTO FILE

Highland ponies and their riders take part in events and shows, especially in Scotland. In Highland ponies, judges expect to see full, flowing manes and soft, silky feathers on the backs of their legs.

MY NOTES & PICTURES

I'VE SEEN...　An adult ◯　A foal ◯

HIGHLAND

The Highland is the largest of all native British ponies. The breed has been developed from wild ponies that lived in Scotland for thousands of years. They were bred to work on farms pulling ploughs and for forestry work, hauling timber. Highland ponies are well suited to cold weather – they are hardy in nature and grow thick winter coats. Modern Highlands have been mixed with Spanish horses and Thoroughbreds, producing ponies with calm natures.

HEIGHT
13–14.2 hh

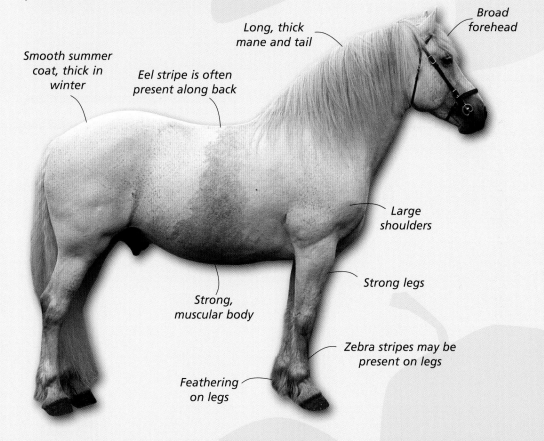

Broad forehead

Long, thick mane and tail

Smooth summer coat, thick in winter

Eel stripe is often present along back

Large shoulders

Strong legs

Strong, muscular body

Zebra stripes may be present on legs

Feathering on legs

IN A... Field ◯   Stable ◯   Show ◯   TV/Film ◯

PONIES

FACT FILE

Place of origin Iceland

Colour Any

Uses Riding, driving, trekking

Characteristics Sure-footed and tough

SUPER FACT

Most horses and ponies move in four gaits: walk, trot, canter and gallop. Icelandics have two extra gaits known as running walk and flying pace.

PHOTO FILE

In parts of Iceland, herds of Icelandic ponies live wild. Others that are owned are turned out in the autumn to live without human interference. Breeders believe this helps to keep the ponies strong.

MY NOTES & PICTURES

I'VE SEEN... An adult   A foal

ICELANDIC

Icelandics are one of several breeds that may be regarded as either ponies or horses. They were first brought to Iceland in the first century AD by the invading Vikings. Later, a law was passed preventing any more horses or ponies being brought onto the island. This allowed a new, pure breed to develop. These ponies are extremely hardy from living outdoors in the freezing conditions of Iceland. Today, Icelandic ponies are used for riding, driving and in competitions.

HEIGHT
12.3–13.2 hh

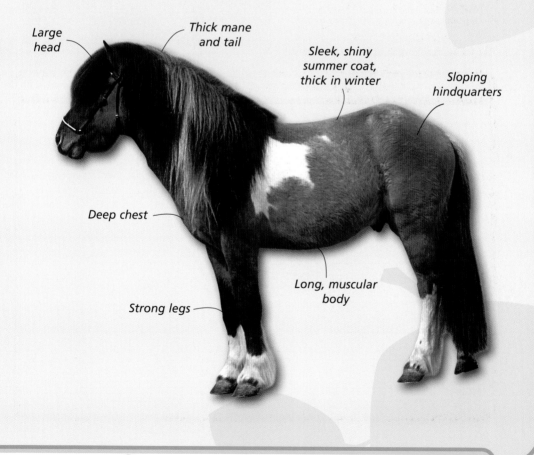

Large head

Thick mane and tail

Sleek, shiny summer coat, thick in winter

Sloping hindquarters

Deep chest

Long, muscular body

Strong legs

IN A... Field ◯   Stable ◯   Show ◯   TV/Film ◯

WARMBLOOD HORSES

FACT FILE

Place of origin Ireland

Colour Any solid colour

Uses Showjumping, hunting, riding

Characteristics Strong and steady

SUPER FACT

Irish Draught horses are excellent jumpers. They are said to have 'hunters' feet' rather than the heavy hooves of their coldblood ancestors.

PHOTO FILE

Irish Draughts compete in cross-country events where both horses and riders need courage, boldness and strength. At these events, solid fences are separated by long stretches of open ground.

MY NOTES & PICTURES

I'VE SEEN...   An adult ◯   A foal ◯

IRISH DRAUGHT

Despite its name, the Irish Draught is a **warmblood horse that is often used for cross-country racing and hunting.** This breed was originally developed for heavy farm work as well as riding. Its ancestors were probably coldbloods mixed with Spanish horses, creating a strong horse with quick movement. The breed nearly died out several times in the past due to their extensive use in World War I (1914–1918) and the mechanization of farm equipment. Today, the Irish Draught is a popular horse.

HEIGHT
15.2–17 hh

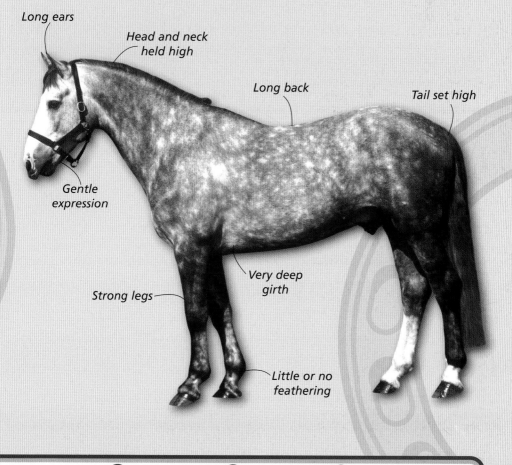

Long ears

Head and neck
held high

Long back

Tail set high

Gentle
expression

Very deep
girth

Strong legs

Little or no
feathering

FACT FILE

Place of origin Lipica, Slovenia

Colour Usually grey, but can be bay

Uses Riding, driving, dressage

Characteristics Intelligent and calm

PHOTO FILE

Grey Lipizzaner stallions at the Spanish Riding School are put through their paces and total obedience is demanded of every horse. The animals and their riders travel the world putting on displays and dazzling shows.

SUPER FACT

This breed was started with just six Spanish stallions that were mated with 24 mares. All of today's Lipizzaners are related to these six males.

MY NOTES & PICTURES

I'VE SEEN... An adult ◯ A foal ◯

LIPIZZANER

The Spanish Riding School in Austria is home to one of the most impressive horse breeds – the Lipizzaner. These fine riding horses were bred at a stud in Lipica in Slovenia 400 years ago. The aim was to develop the world's finest horses by breeding Spanish horses with other breeds, including Arabs. Lipizzaners are lively, have great grace and are fast to learn. They are trained to pull carriages and perform a huge range of movements, including leaps and advanced dressage.

HEIGHT
15.1–16.2 hh

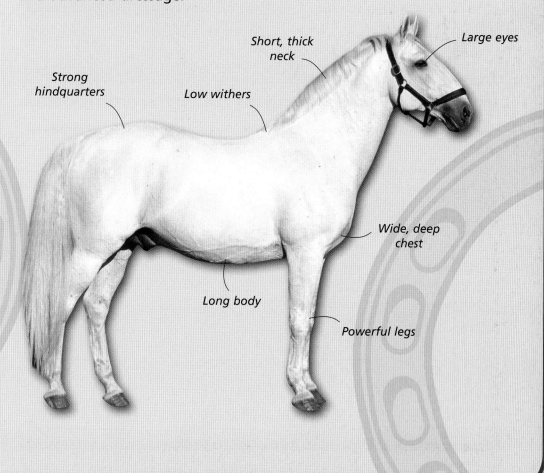

Short, thick neck

Large eyes

Strong hindquarters

Low withers

Wide, deep chest

Long body

Powerful legs

WARMBLOOD HORSES

FACT FILE

Place of origin Eastern USA

Colour Bay, brown, chestnut or black

Uses Riding, driving

Characteristics Intelligent and good-natured

SUPER FACT

Morgans have played an important role in developing many American breeds, including the Quarter Horse and the Tennessee Walking Horse.

PHOTO FILE

This Morgan stallion displays the elegance of the breed. Long tails and manes are common, adding to their beauty. Morgans that are most similar to the early members of the breed are called 'Foundation Morgans'.

MY NOTES & PICTURES

I'VE SEEN... An adult 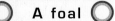 A foal

MORGAN

The Morgan – possibly the first breed to be developed in America – descended from a stallion called Justin Morgan. This original Morgan is thought to have been a mix of Arab and Thoroughbred and was named after its owner. The breed became famous for its abilities to work hard on the farm as well as for competing successfully in shows. Morgans are known for their gentle, affectionate natures.

HEIGHT
14.1–15.1 hh

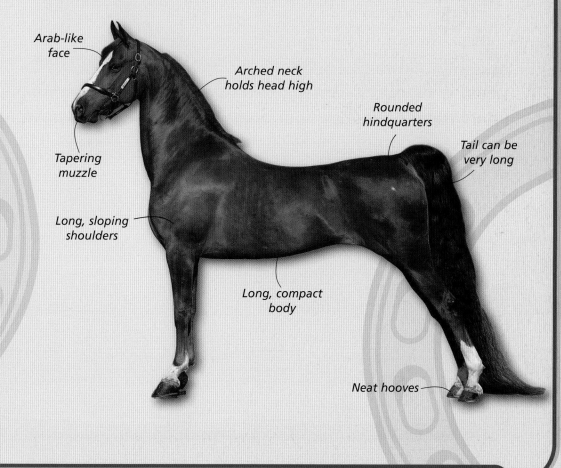

Arab-like face

Arched neck holds head high

Rounded hindquarters

Tail can be very long

Tapering muzzle

Long, sloping shoulders

Long, compact body

Neat hooves

WARMBLOOD HORSES

FACT FILE

Place of origin Western USA

Colour Any colour, but brown, bay and chestnut are common

Uses Cattle herding

Characteristics Hardy and unpredictable

SUPER FACT

Due to interbreeding with many other breeds, Mustangs can be almost any colour and they also vary a great deal in size. One Mustang reached 18 hands high.

PHOTO FILE

Mustangs live in herds in the wild. They are not true wild horses as they are descended from horses that were domesticated. Their name comes from a Spanish word meaning 'a horse with no owner'.

MY NOTES & PICTURES

I'VE SEEN...   An adult ◯   A foal ◯

MUSTANG

Mustangs are tough, wild warmblood **horses of the United States.** They are descended from Spanish horses that were brought over by Europeans in the 16th century. By the 1900s there was a huge population of Mustangs roaming North America. People began hunting and killing the horses at an alarming rate and by the 1970s Mustangs had suffered a serious drop in numbers. Today, these wild horses are protected by US law.

HEIGHT
13–16 hh

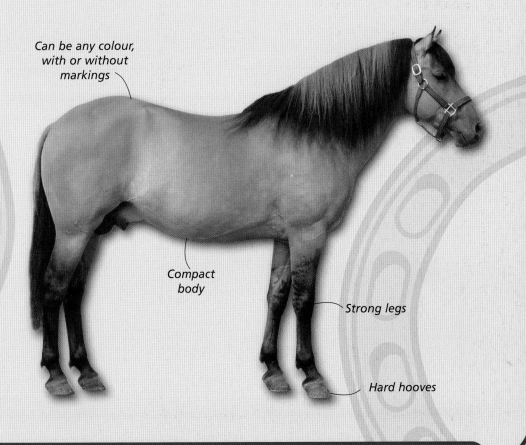

Can be any colour, with or without markings

Compact body

Strong legs

Hard hooves

PONIES

FACT FILE

Place of origin England

Colour Any, except piebald or skewbald

Uses Riding, dressage, hunting, showing

Characteristics Fast and friendly

SUPER FACT

All New Forest ponies that roam wild have owners. Their owners are known as 'commoners' and they pay a small fee to leave their ponies in the woodland.

PHOTO FILE

New Forest ponies get their name from the woodland area in Hampshire, England, where they have roamed free for many years. They graze without being fed by humans, even through the winter when food is scarce.

MY NOTES & PICTURES

I'VE SEEN...   An adult ◯   A foal ◯

NEW FOREST

This breed is one of the most adaptable of all ponies – New Forest ponies suit riding, jumping, hunting, dressage, cross-country, polo and much more! They respond well to people and are easy to ride. These ponies originally come from the woodlands of the New Forest in southern England where they have lived for at least 1000 years. Around 100 years ago, the breed was improved by introducing Arab and Thoroughbred blood.

HEIGHT
12.2–14.2 hh

Strong, muscular hindquarters

Arched neck

Short back

Large head

Sloping shoulders

Straight legs

Hard hooves

IN A... Field ◯   Stable ◯   Show ◯   TV/Film ◯

COLDBLOOD HORSES

FACT FILE

Place of origin Northern France

Colour Grey or black

Uses Farm work, pulling, showing

Characteristics Elegant and hard-working

SUPER FACT

One of the world's tallest horses was a Percheron called Dr Le Gear. He was born in 1902 and his adult height was 21 hands high – around 2.13 metres.

PHOTO FILE

After World War II (1939–1945), the number of Percherons dropped to double figures. Since then, the breed has become popular again. These large horses work well in teams pulling carriages and heavy loads.

MY NOTES & PICTURES

I'VE SEEN... An adult ◯ A foal ◯

PERCHERON

These coldblood horses get their name from the region in northern France where they were first developed – La Perche. Percherons originate from local horses being bred with Arabs brought to France by invaders in the eighth century AD. Adding Arab blood to the breed produced powerful horses with good movement and an elegant appearance. Percherons have little or no feathering, which means their legs stay clean while working in the fields.

HEIGHT
16.1–17.1 hh

Thick mane

Broad forehead

Sloping hindquarters

Large eyes

Fine coat

Sloping shoulders

Body is deep through the girth

Short, powerful legs

Little or no feathers

IN A... Field ◯   Stable ◯   Show ◯   TV/Film ◯

WARMBLOOD HORSES

FACT FILE

Place of origin Mongolia

Colour Dun with black points

Uses Wild

Characteristics Tough and sturdy

SUPER FACT

There were around four primitive types of horse alive 10,000 years ago. Przewalski's Horse and the Tarpan are the only two that survive today.

PHOTO FILE

Thick fur on their legs and bodies help Przewalski's Horses to survive the winter. These horses became extinct in the wild in the 1970s. Now many are being bred in zoos and conservation parks to save the breed.

MY NOTES & PICTURES

I'VE SEEN...   An adult ◯   A foal ◯

PRZEWALSKI'S HORSE

These wild, sand-coloured horses were named by a Russian explorer called Nicolai Przewalski in the 1870s. Przewalski's Horses have existed in Europe and Asia for thousands of years. Their numbers dropped dramatically as people and other animals took over their habitat. This forced the wild herds to the edge of the Gobi Desert, in Mongolia. Now Przewalksi's Horses are protected in reserves where they are encouraged to breed.

HEIGHT
12–14.2 hh

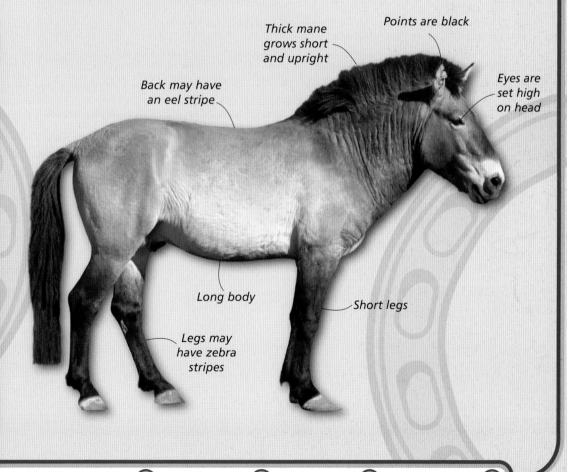

Thick mane grows short and upright

Points are black

Back may have an eel stripe

Eyes are set high on head

Long body

Short legs

Legs may have zebra stripes

WARMBLOOD HORSES

FACT FILE

Place of origin Virginia, USA

Colour Any solid colour

Uses Riding, cattle herding, racing, rodeo

Characteristics Agile and intelligent

SUPER FACT

Quarter Horses have been called the world's favourite horse – there are more than three million of them registered in the USA alone.

PHOTO FILE

Quarter Horses are well known for their use in rodeos. Horses need to be able to start, stop and turn at speed. At these events, cowboys and cowgirls display their skills in roping calves and agility riding.

MY NOTES & PICTURES

I'VE SEEN...   An adult   A foal

QUARTER HORSE

Quarter Horses were first bred in the United States more than 300 years ago. During the week they were used for farm work and riding, and at the weekends they were run in races. The races were conducted on a track a quarter of a mile (402 metres) long, which is how these horses got their name. Quarter Horses could outrun other breeds in these sprint races, reaching speeds of around 80 kilometres per hour. They are now bred for racing, cattle herding and for use in rodeos.

HEIGHT
14–16 hh

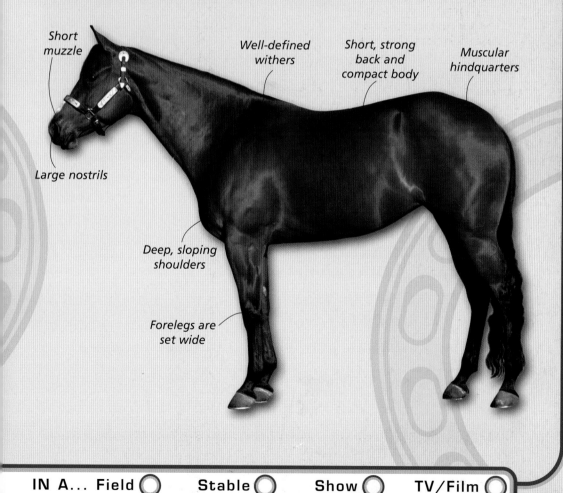

Short muzzle

Well-defined withers

Short, strong back and compact body

Muscular hindquarters

Large nostrils

Deep, sloping shoulders

Forelegs are set wide

IN A... Field ◯   Stable ◯   Show ◯   TV/Film ◯

PONIES

FACT FILE

Place of origin Shetland Isles, Scotland

Colour Any

Uses Driving, riding, showing

Characteristics Strong and intelligent

PHOTO FILE

These ponies and their riders are taking part in the Shetland Pony Grand National. Young jockeys are dressed in silks, like jockeys in the real Grand National. The ponies have to clear small jumps around the course.

SUPER FACT

Shetlands are measured in inches not hands. For a Shetland pony to be registered in the breed stud book, it should not exceed 42 inches in height.

MY NOTES & PICTURES

I'VE SEEN... An adult ◯ A foal ◯

SHETLAND

Little Shetland ponies are hugely popular around the world. They are one of the world's smallest breeds so can only be ridden by children. However, Shetlands are very strong and are often used for driving and pulling small carriages. These ponies originate from the Shetland Isles off the northeast coast of Scotland, where they have lived for thousands of years. The long, cold winters of this region have resulted in an extremely hardy breed. Many Shetlands were used for ploughing and as pit ponies during the 1800s, before becoming popular as children's riding ponies.

HEIGHT
Up to 42 inches
(107 cm)

Small ears

Large eyes

Sleek summer coat, thick in winter

Full tail

Neat head

Deep body

Short legs

COLDBLOOD HORSES

FACT FILE

Place of origin England

Colour Brown, bay, black or grey

Uses Farm work, pulling, showing

Characteristics Powerful and friendly

SUPER FACT

The Shire is named after the English counties, such as Cambridgeshire, Derbyshire, Leicestershire and Lincolnshire, where it worked on farms.

PHOTO FILE

These Shires are harnessed and decorated for a show. They wear rows of horse brasses, which have traditionally been used to decorate their harnesses as far back as the 1600s.

MY NOTES & PICTURES

I'VE SEEN... An adult A foal

SHIRE

The beautiful Shire is one of the most famous coldbloods. These tall horses were developed to work on farms, at docks and to help with the building of the railways. Their history goes back to Medieval times when powerful horses were needed to carry soldiers in heavy suits of armour into battle. Shire horse numbers, like many coldbloods, declined as tractors became common during the last century. Shires are often seen at British agricultural fairs and shows, but they are exported around the world.

HEIGHT
16.2–17.2 hh

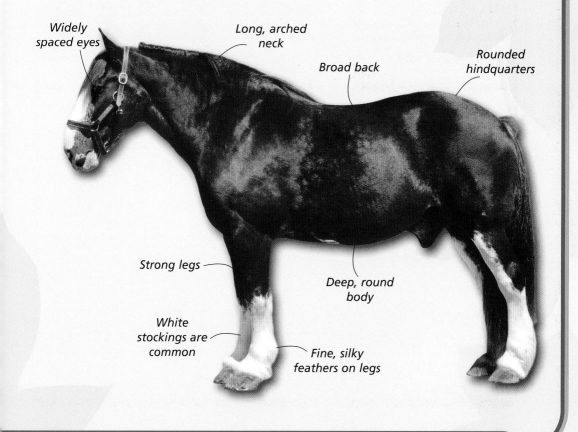

Widely spaced eyes

Long, arched neck

Broad back

Rounded hindquarters

Strong legs

Deep, round body

White stockings are common

Fine, silky feathers on legs

COLDBLOOD HORSES

FACT FILE

Place of origin Suffolk, England

Colour Chestnut, sometimes with white markings on face

Uses Farm work, showing

Characteristics Gentle and tough

SUPER FACT

Every Suffolk alive today shares a common ancestor – a stallion called Crisp's Horse of Ufford, which was born in 1768.

PHOTO FILE

Horses at shows are groomed and decorated to look their best. Adult Suffolk Punches have their manes and tails plaited. Ribbons and tassels are woven into the plait for colour. Foals should have natural manes and tails.

MY NOTES & PICTURES

I'VE SEEN...　An adult 　A foal

SUFFOLK

The Suffolk, also known as the Suffolk Punch, has had a difficult history. It was first bred around 500 years ago for agricultural work. The breed became particularly popular for its ability to work for long hours on little food. Numbers declined when machines took over the tasks they traditionally performed on the farm. New breeders have helped to save the Suffolk, but these horses are still rare and make welcome appearances at shows.

HEIGHT
16–17 hh

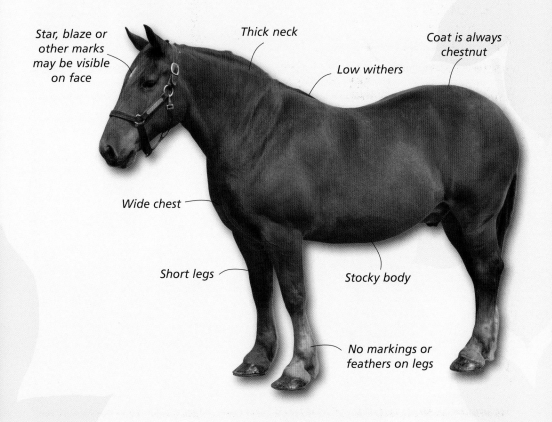

Star, blaze or other marks may be visible on face

Thick neck

Low withers

Coat is always chestnut

Wide chest

Short legs

Stocky body

No markings or feathers on legs

WARMBLOOD HORSES

FACT FILE

Place of origin Sweden

Colour Any solid colour

Uses Riding, showjumping, dressage, eventing

Characteristics Good-natured and clever

SUPER FACT

Swedish Warmbloods are rigorously inspected to decide if they can breed. This careful inspection process ensures the high quality of the breed.

PHOTO FILE

Swedish Warmbloods are bred to produce championship showjumpers. They must be able to change direction at speed, leap over the highest obstacles and complete the course against the clock.

MY NOTES & PICTURES

I'VE SEEN...   An adult ◯   A foal ◯

SWEDISH WARMBLOOD

Crossing local Swedish horses with those brought over from other parts of Europe helped to develop the breed now known as the **Swedish Warmblood.** These horses are elegant, with the toughness of the small Swedish horses. They are now famous as excellent competition horses and can be trained to take part in many events, such as showjumping, dressage and driving. Swedish Warmbloods often compete at the Olympic Games, but are as popular with amateur riders as they are with professionals.

HEIGHT
16.2–17 hh

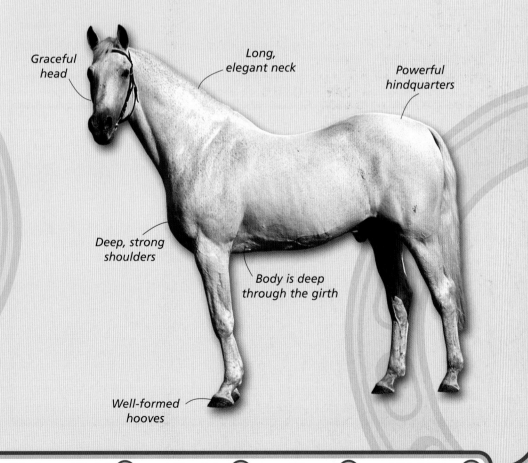

Graceful head

Long, elegant neck

Powerful hindquarters

Deep, strong shoulders

Body is deep through the girth

Well-formed hooves

IN A... Field ◯   Stable ◯   Show ◯   TV/Film ◯

HOTBLOOD HORSES

FACT FILE

Place of origin England

Colour Solid colours, such as brown, bay, chestnut and grey

Uses Riding, racing, showing, dressage

Characteristics Athletic and high-spirited

SUPER FACT

All Thoroughbreds can be traced back to one of three stallions used to start the breed – the Darley Arabian, the Godolphin Arabian and the Byerly Turk.

PHOTO FILE

Many Thoroughbreds have become well-known as successful race horses. The Thoroughbred Red Rum is the only horse to have won the Grand National three times, winning in 1973, 1974 and 1977.

MY NOTES & PICTURES

I'VE SEEN... An adult ◯ A foal ◯

THOROUGHBRED

Thoroughbreds have been bred for their **impressive speed.** Not only are they the fastest horses in the world, they are also widely regarded as the finest riding horses. Thoroughbreds are extremely intelligent and are quick to learn and respond to commands. They were first produced in England around 300 years ago by mating three Arab stallions with English mares. Thoroughbreds are often crossed with other breeds to improve them.

HEIGHT
15.2–16.2 hh

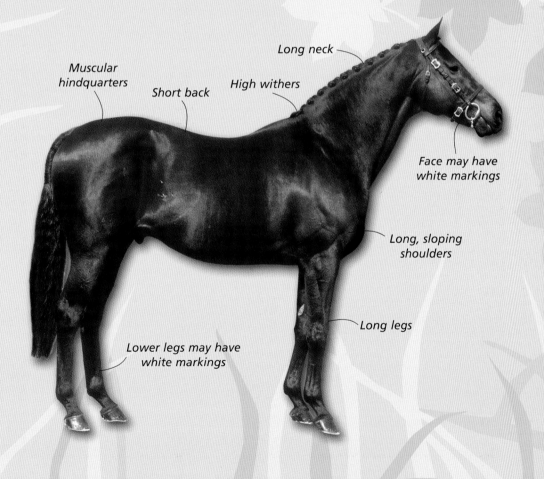

Long neck

Muscular hindquarters

Short back

High withers

Face may have white markings

Long, sloping shoulders

Long legs

Lower legs may have white markings

PONIES

FACT FILE

Place of origin Wales

Colour Any

Uses Riding, eventing, showing

Characteristics Good-natured and strong

SUPER FACT

The four types of Welsh pony are Section A – Welsh Mountain Pony, Section B – Welsh Pony, Section C – Welsh Pony of Cob Type and Section D – Welsh Cob.

PHOTO FILE

Welsh Ponies often compete successfully in shows because they combine intelligence and obedience with beauty. They are taller than Section A ponies and their long legs are ideal for riding at faster speeds.

MY NOTES & PICTURES

I'VE SEEN... An adult ◯ A foal ◯

WELSH SECTION B

The Welsh Section B, also known as the Welsh Pony, has Arab ancestors. It is thought that Welsh Mountain Ponies (Section A) were also bred with Hackneys and Thoroughbreds to create this modern breed. This produced an intelligent pony with long legs, making it ideal for riding. Welsh Ponies move with elegance and have great agility. They often compete in gymkhanas and other competition events.

HEIGHT
12.2–13.2 hh

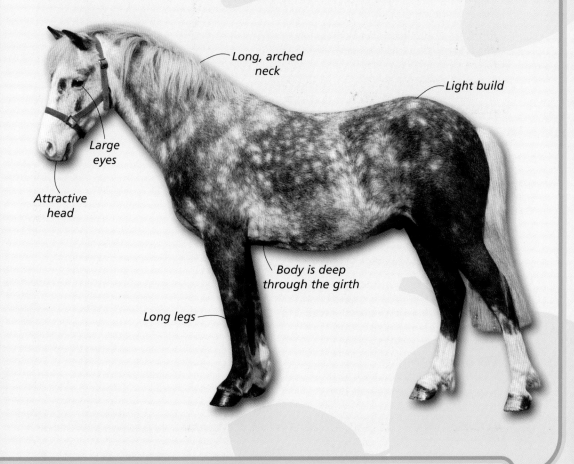

Long, arched neck

Light build

Large eyes

Attractive head

Body is deep through the girth

Long legs

IN A... Field ○   Stable ○   Show ○   TV/Film ○

FINDING OUT MORE

EQUESTRIAN CLUBS AND ORGANIZATIONS

If you want to get involved with horses and ponies why not contact your local riding school – you may be able to help them out in your free time. There are also equestrian clubs and organizations that you might like to become a member of.

The British Equestrian Federation **http://www.bef.co.uk**
The British Horse Society **http://www.bhs.org.uk**
The Pony Club **http://www.pcuk.org**

EQUESTRIAN MAGAZINES

British Dressage **http://www.britishdressage.co.uk**
Horse **http://www.horsemagazine.co.uk**
Horse and Hound **http://www.horseandhound.co.uk**
Horse and Pony **http://www.horseandpony.com**
Just Dressage **http://www.just-dressage.co.uk**
Your Horse **http://www.yourhorse.co.uk**

WEBSITES

Try these websites for lots of interesting information and facts about horses and ponies as well as games, pictures and things to do.

http://www.my-horse-club.com
http://www.newrider.com
http://www.britisheventing.com
http://www.horsedrivingtrials.co.uk
http://www.equine-world.co.uk
http://www.equestrian.co.uk
http://www.hoys.co.uk
http://www.equiworld.net
http://www.horseworlddata.com
http://www.factsforprojects.com

GLOSSARY

Coldbloods Large, heavy horses from northern Europe, often used for pulling loads.

Colic Abdominal pain.

Conformation The shape and build of a horse or pony.

Deep through the girth A good measurement from the withers to the elbow. This is desirable in conformation because it shows there is plenty of room for the lungs to expand.

Dressage The training of a horse or pony to develop obedience and to perform special movements.

Driving When horses or ponies are hitched up to vehicles, such as carts or carriages, and driven in shows and races.

Eventing A sport in which competitors take part in cross-country, dressage and showjumping over three days.

Equid Any animal in the horse family.

Feathers In horses and ponies, the long hairs that grow on the lower legs.

Foal A young horse or pony.

Gait The way that a horse or pony moves.

Girth The strap that goes around a horse's or pony's belly to hold the saddle in place.

Gymkhana An event where horses and ponies, and their riders, take part in several competitions.

Hands high (hh) The unit that a horse's or pony's height is measured in. One hand is equal to 10 cm.

Herd A large group of animals that live together.

Hindquarters The back end of a horse or pony including its hind legs.

Hotbloods Pure-bred, high-spirited horses, known for their speed.

Mare A female horse or pony, four years old or more.

Mitbah The angle at which the head meets the neck in Arabian horses.

Muzzle The area around a horse's or pony's mouth and nose.

Points of a horse The parts of a horse's or pony's anatomy.

Polo A team game played on horseback. Players score by hitting a small ball with a long-handled mallet into the opposing team's goal.

Show An event where horses or ponies are judged on their conformation and movement.

Stallion A male horse or pony, four years old or more.

Stamina The ability to sustain physical effort for a long time.

Stud book A book containing a list of all the registered pedigree animals of a breed.

Temperament The nature and behaviour of a horse or pony.

Turn out To let a horse or pony loose in a field or paddock.

Warmbloods Calm and sturdy horses that can run at speed.

ACKNOWLEDGEMENTS

All artwork is from the Miles Kelly Artwork Bank

The publishers would like to thank the following sources
for the use of their photographs:

Alamy 32 Bruce Coleman Inc.

Bob Langrish 20, 21, 22, 23, 24, 25, 27, 28, 29, 31, 33, 36, 37, 38,
39, 41, 42, 43, 45, 46, 47, 48, 49, 51, 53, 54, 55, 56, 57, 59, 61, 62, 63, 65, 66, 67,
68, 69, 70, 71, 73, 75, 76, 77, 81, 82, 83, 85, 86, 87, 88, 89, 91, 92, 93

FLPA 34 Sunset; 78 Terry Whittaker; 80 Terry Whittaker

Fotolia.com 13(t) Alexandre, (b) Anita Zander; 14(br) Michael Bravo; 16(t) Swanlake;
17(t) simonkr; 60 Bernd Meiseberg; 64 boris verseghy; 74 hkfoto; 79 StarJumper

Rex Features 35 Timo Jaakonaho

Shutterstock.com Cover Groomee

All other photographs from:
digitalSTOCK, digitalvision, iStock.com, John Foxx, PhotoAlto,
PhotoDisc, PhotoEssentials, PhotoPro, Stockbyte